The Go-Getter

Susan M. Fenton Willoughby

Pacific Press Publishing Association
Boise, Idaho
Montemorelos, Nuevo Leon, Mexico
Oshawa, Ontario, Canada

Designed by Tim Larson
Cover Illustration by Eric Joyner

Copyright © 1985 by
Pacific Press Publishing Association
Printed in United States of America
All Rights Reserved

Library of Congress Cataloging in Publication Data

Willoughby, Susan M. Fenton
   The go-getter.

   Bibliography: p.
   1. Success. 2. Christian life—Seventh-Day Adventist authors.
I. Title.
BJ1611.2.W466   1985   158'.1   85-3591

ISBN 0-8163-0604-4

85 86 87 88 89 • 6 5 4 3 2 1

Contents

Success Is Within Your Grasp

That you have begun to read this volume
shows that you have experienced
a measure of success.
The Go-Getter will enable you to—
keep moving forward as you surmount
   obstacles and remove barriers;
look at yourself in a positive light;
know that success is not only in being on
   top but is also in climbing;
recognize that success is not reserved
   only for individuals with ten talents—
   that developing one talent to its
   fullest is also being successful.

Introduction

The name of this volume has been borrowed from the title of a poem—"The Go-Getter"—which I learned as a child. I have never seen this poem in print, but learned it while my mother, the late Mrs. Mabel Fenton of Montserrat, West Indies, was teaching it to my older sister. "The Go-Getter" has ever since been a challenge to me. I have shared it with audiences in many lands and, according to the reports, the lives of many young people have been positively influenced by it. I now share the poem with you (thanks to the unknown author).

The Go-Getter

The Go-getter goes till he gets what he goes for.
The Go-getter works till he reaps what he sows for.
He fixes a goal and resolves when he sets it,
The way to the prize is to go till he gets it.

The country is crowded with weakling diminishers.
And plastered with want-ads for resolute finishers.
It's easy enough to start things with a roar
But hard to keep pulling when biceps are sore.

There's many an auto equipped with a starter
That starts up the hill like the charge of a tartar,
But soon it is found, it has also a stopper.
The auto we need is the one with a topper.

The highway of life has a hundred who peter,
To one who will stick and become a repeater.
To seer and to dreamer the world is a debtor—
But passes it's handsome gift to the getter.

The Go-getter goes till he gets what he goes for.
The Go-getter works till he reaps what he sows for.
He fixes a goal and resolves when he sets it,
The way to the prize is to go till he gets it.

"Go-getter" is a kinetic term which implies potential and suggests movement. Movement *to* where assumes movement *from* where. Go-getters need to evaluate their positions in order to understand what thrust they might have for their pursuit.

Among the first lessons that Go-getters learn is that they must begin right where they are. Individuals often encounter many problems because they do not take time to evaluate their starting position. "Begin Where You Are." This advice will be further developed in chapter one.

Since Go-getters know they will reap what they sow, they will want to sow the seeds that will produce the fruit they desire; they will choose wisely their direction. They will find out what is needed and then move in the right direction toward fulfilling that need. Nothing is more embarrassing than for a big, strong man to help a little old lady across a busy street that she didn't wish to cross. Chapter two—"Use What You've Got"—discusses using what you've got to go in the right direction.

To succeed you must use what you've got. Perhaps you have heard the story by Raymond Sill, "Hero and the Coward".[1] The coward stood at the edge of the battle looking at his sword, saying, "What can I do with this old sword?" I can almost hear him saying, "If only I had a better blade, a sharper blade, I could be of some help. I suppose the Prince up there has a real steel blade in his sword." Disgusted, he snapped his sword over his knee and broke it in two pieces. He then threw them in the sand and ran from the battlefield. But the hero—the Prince—to whom the coward had referred, had no sword at all. He had lost it in the battle. In fact, the Prince was fighting with his bare hands. At one point, as the enemies were pushing him back with their spears, he stumbled over the hilt of the coward's broken sword. He reached down, pulled it out of the sand, held it high in the air, and with a shout, charged like a king. His soldiers saw him charging with a broken sword, and they rallied around him. They won not only the battle, but they won the war. Go-getters know that to succeed they must use what they have, and you will read more about this in chapter two.

According to the coward in the above story, "if only he had the Prince's sword; if only his sword had a steel blade," he would have worked wonders. Well, the Go-getter can accomplish more with half a sword than some can accomplish with a whole sword. One reason is that *If* is not a part of the Go-getters vocabulary—and "*If* Is Not a Part of Your Vocabulary." Read more about this in chapter three.

Go-getters not only avoid such words as *If*—they also refuse to allow a negative mental attitude to replace a positive one. When Go-getters are faced with a barrier, they face it and press forward, because for them "*Never* Is Not a Word." (See chapter four.) At the same time, Go-getters recognize that detours occasionally have to be made. They recognize the difference between the signs "Road Closed" and "Detour." Go-getters are not afraid to use alternative paths to achieve their goals. They also know that their best is enough. "Your Best Is Enough" is the focus of chapter five.

In the King James Version of the Bible, 2 Kings 6, is an account of the sons of the prophets who requested of Elisha that they work together to build a larger dwelling place. Elisha agreed, but one man ran into trouble (verses 5, 6): "But as one was felling a beam, the axe head fell into the water: and he cried, and said, Alas, master! for it was borrowed. And the man of God said, Where fell it? And he shewed him the place. And he cut down a stick, and 'cast it in thither; and the iron did swim." God provided a way for the task to be continued and completed. "Though he fall, he shall not be utterly cast down: for the Lord upholdeth him with his hand."[2]

In your home, your school, your church, your community—no matter to what group you belong—intelligent, caring people expect no more from you than your best.

And you will be able to begin where you are, using what you've got, and accomplishing your best, because for you *If* and *Never* are foreign terms. Why? Because you know how to place "JESUS FIRST" and thus realize many successes. This is the message of chapter six.

Since there is no map for Go-getters and since Go-getters and their goals differ widely, a short "How-to" chapter concludes this book—a chapter entitled "Recipes."

Foreword

The writer of this stimulating and challenging volume speaks from the wealth of her own experience. I have known her for nearly forty years, and well remember when it was my good fortune to hear her recite "The Go-Getter" at one of our school functions. I believe Dr. Willoughby is well qualified, both by experience and example, to write this inspirational challenge to all of us as her readers—old, middle-aged, and young alike.

As you read this book, you will catch a little of the indomitable spirit that has activated her from her youngest days in elementary school and on through academy, college, and university,. She has simply refused to allow any obstacle of man or nature to keep her down. Her spirit of achievement is contagious. "Plus Ultra"—"More Beyond," have long been her mottoes. "Where there's a will, there's a way." "Not poverty, but low aim is the crime." "Nothing succeeds like success."

Phrase it as you will, it all comes out the same—Never give up! Keep on keeping-on. Let nothing get you down. This has been the constant precept of her life.

Her love affair with life, as seen in her accomplishments, has touched thousands of lives. Teaching and speaking in schools and churches, at crowded campmeetings, and in sophisticated gatherings, her message is always the same. "The Go-getter goes till he gets what he goes for."

Let us have no whining and blaming of people, place, or circumstances. Fate may sometimes seem to conspire against us, and the crushing circumstances of life may deal us some terrible blows—and when this happens lesser mortals may be tempted to roll over and die. "Don't," says the author. "Get up and continue fighting. The darkest hour is just before the dawn."

Dr. Willoughby, like most of her fellow students in the early days, came from humble surroundings. She was taught by her parents the value of being content with little, and the scriptural truth that "a man's life consisteth not in the abundance of the things which he possesseth" (Luke 12:15) became a practical, living principle. With this basic philosophy anchored in her thinking, she pursued every opportunity to expand her horizons, to climb the educational ladder, and to snatch ultimate victory from the hungry jaws of defeat.

From elementary school in Montserrat and Antigua, through secondary school in Trinidad, on to college and a bachelor's degree at Atlantic Union College in Massachussetts, she pursued her dream. With some detours along the way—including marriage and children—she determined nonetheless to reach the top of the educational ladder. She proceeded to finish two master's degrees and finally a doctoral degree from Harvard University, the queen of the Ivy League Schools. Harvard—a long way from the little elementary school in Antigua!

Dr. Willoughby continues sharing her philosophy of life with her students and continues also to pursue postgraduate studies—"For the Go-getter goes till he gets what he goes for."

G. Ralph Thompson, Secretary
General Conference of Seventh-day Adventists

Begin
Where You Are

"Whatsoever thy hand findeth to do, do it with thy might."[3]

> Do not wait until some deed of greatness you may do
> Do not wait to shine your light afar
> To the many duties ever near you now be true
> Brighten the corner where you are.[4]

Ina Duley Ogdon may have had you in mind when she wrote those words. It is human nature for individuals to want to perform great feats—to want to be the best. But often it is difficult to find many who take pleasure in enduring the rigors of rehearsal or the long hours of practice—whether preparing the lungs for the opera or preparing the legs for the hundred-yard dash.

So though you have the spirit of a Go-getter, you may yet need to do some self-assessment. Which means that you must be aware of where you are—either in physical location or in your level of attainment—and then decide where you want to go. You must set a goal, or probably several goals. Some writers suggest setting one main goal and several subgoals.

Whichever procedure you prefer, remember that the first step is of utmost importance. What is so important about a step? A step denotes direction. In doing your self-assessment, you will not only want to set your goal but also plan the direction you will take. Therefore the personal guidelines you develop can later serve as guideposts and will assist you in rating your progress.

In this chapter let us perform four functions:

1. Assessment of self
2. Establishment of goals
3. Choice of direction
4. Development of guidelines

Assessment of Self

The next line is for you. Read it aloud and listen to your voice: *"What do I think of myself this very moment?"* If you think you have potential, who is anybody to tell you that you don't?

In assessing yourself, you need to think of some things in life that you have done well. Then think of some other things you have done, but not as well. This process will help you recognize that there is room for improvement and that you are willing to admit it. Then you must exercise confidence in your abilities to get to the top. A little adage says:

> *If you can imagine it, you can become it.*
> *If you can dream it, you can be it.*

A boy once heard of a job opening in a department store. Applicants were to be at the store the next morning when the store opened—at eight o'clock. This little boy was there on time, but he found twenty other boys in line ahead of him. However, he didn't get discouraged, and he didn't become disgusted and return home. No—he had confidence in himself and enthusiasm to go along with his confidence.

He scribbled a note, rushed to the head of the line where the secretary was taking names, gave her the note, and said, "Would you please give this to the boss at once. It is very urgent that he see it immediately!"

The boss saw the boyish scrawl and read these words: "I'm the twenty-first kid in line. Don't hire anyone until you see me!" Well, he got the job! Who wouldn't want a boy who had that spark? You must have confidence. You must "dream the impossible dream." That little boy's goal was to get that job—and get it he did. What is *your* goal?

Establishment of Goals

Most of us have read this statement by Robert Browning: "A man's reach should exceed his grasp." Yes, today's accomplishment is the foundation for tomorrow's achievements. What you will be, you are now becoming. Remember that progress is never stagnant. You must have a goal if you are to avoid much activity without accomplishment.

I can't remember when my actions were without goals, whether that goal was relaxation, passing an examination, or closing a sale. As a student in a Seventh-day Adventist school in St. John's, Antigua, West Indies, I solicited funds for "Harvest Ingathering" on my way to and from school. The school had a goal—so each student had a goal which was a subgoal of the school's. However, any student could set a personal goal which exceeded the given goal. I had my personal goal.

One midday as I was returning to school, I met two well-dressed businessmen on the street and decided to walk along with them and tell them about the program of which I was a part. I told them that we solicited funds and sent that money overseas to help the needy. I concluded by saying, "I am sure you will want to contribute." I smiled, they smiled, and they contributed. The contribution was much greater than average. In fact, it was the largest I had received, so I made certain they signed my "permission card" and indicated the amount of each contribution.

Overjoyed, and still on my way to attend afternoon classes, I approached another businessman in his office and concluded my speech in the same fashion. In addition, however, I presented my "permission card" for his signature before he reached for his contribution. Naturally, his amount was no less than that of the last two. The trend was set. I recognized what the power of suggestion could do. My goal was no longer to raise the amount of money assigned me, or even to raise my personal goal, but to raise the class goal—and I succeeded.

Later, in Trinidad, I raised half of what was assigned the church. In New York City I raised the youth goal— and the church sent me to San Francisco to the Youth Congress as a sign of their appreciation.

There are levels of attainment, and incremental steps are important. After you have completed one step of your ladder, move on to a higher step. But understand that you must "Begin Where You Are."

Out of Irish mythology comes a story of a farmer who was given a series of almost impossible tasks to perform—one of which was to bring in by sunset all the seeds sown in a certain field, else he could not achieve the desires of his heart.

When even came he was still far from completing the task. Suddenly an army of ants came to his rescue. Each of them came rushing in, carrying a seed. By sunset all the seeds were in except one. The man was terrified, lest this mean he had lost his chance for happiness. But before

the sun went down, one last lame ant came limping in
with the final missing seed.

As Patrick Mahoney so aptly puts it, "Some of us are at
best but lame ants, but as long as we aspire to some goal
in life, we shall get there before the sun sets." [5]

What kind of career goal have you set for yourself? In
developing a plan to reach that goal, you will need to ask
yourself several questions. For example, *what* do I really
want to do? *Why* do I want to do it? *How* am I going to
accomplish it—what plans do I have? And *where* should
my preparation begin? (That "where" might include the
educational institutions you should consider.)

Choice of Direction

> When you awoke from sleep this morning,
> Though the hour was rather late,
> Did you stop to speak with Jesus
> And His benediction wait?
> Did you tell him that you'd gladly
> Go wherever He would lead—
> That you'd try to do His bidding,
> Helping every soul in need?
> —Author Unknown

The most lasting and sound plans are the ones made as
you keep in mind pleasing God. I am fortunate that I had
parents interested in pleasing God, and I have followed in
their footsteps. Many of my friends and acquaintances
have asked questions that I have been unable to answer.
"What do you think you would have been doing now if—
instead of attending a one-room Seventh-day Adventist
church school—your parents had allowed you to continue
in the public school where you were earmarked to be the
island scholar?" "Where do you think you would be now

if, after you passed the state examination, you had accepted the state scholarship and had gone to a state school free of charge for four years instead of becoming a literature evangelist in order to attend Atlantic Union College?" I still don't have answers to those questions. One thing I do know is that I am exactly where God wants me to be, doing just what He wants me to do.

My plans have not always turned out the way I would have liked or expected. I have endured disappointments, suffered hardships, experienced setbacks, taken detours—but that which has kept me always inching upward has been the knowledge that in making any plan I had stopped to speak with Jesus and in my humanity had listened to His voice.

In developing your plans, you need to remember that there are two ways for travelers—only two ways—and that once you have decided to choose the Jesus way you will be satisfied with your choice.

I remember my first off-campus job in the "real" world. My typing and shorthand speed had so far surpassed that of the other applicants that without completing other necessary forms I was immediately ushered into the boss's office and asked to begin to work right away. For this reason I did not know at first that the job was six days a week, Monday through Saturday. My boss, who was the head of the company, worked parts of six days a week and did not want to deal with more than one secretary. His secretary could have typists and would never be overworked, but he wanted that secretary to be in the office when he was there.

My job interview had been held on a Wednesday, so Wednesday was my first day on the job. Not until Friday were Saturday activities mentioned. My decision had to be made right there and then—and alone. My mother had always been in the habit of praying me through my examinations. She would say, "You must do all that is humanly possible in your preparation and then leave the rest to Jesus."

But today she didn't know about this decision. And was I ever tempted! This was the best secretarial position in the whole industry. Later, I could receive the title of executive secretary, have my own secretary, and be in charge of the typing pool. Success was knocking earlier than I had expected. As I struggled, the text kept coming to my mind: "There hath no temptation taken you but such as is common to man: but God . . . will . . . make a way to escape."

With God's help I made my choice and decided not to work Sabbaths. I have never regretted it. Later I was offered a job as executive secretary to the Secretary of the Medical Board of Trinidad and Tobago. God used me there to save the medical work of my church—a work then in its infancy. The power of choice is a great gift, and making the right choice is crucial as we plan the direction we would like our lives to take. The world is constantly changing; so there is no permanent guide that will serve for all time. However, developing guidelines indeed facilitates success.

Development of Guidelines

To succeed you need not only to know where you are (assessment), where you want to go (goal), and what directions you wish to take to get there (plans)—but you also need some method of evaluation, some kind of progress chart to encourage you by showing your accomplishments. Such a chart tells you how far you have come and inspires you to continue toward your goal.

These are your guidelines. You are now ready to "Use What You've Got."

Use What You've Got

"The spider taketh hold with her hands, and is in kings' palaces." [6]

In the Commonwealth of Massachusetts, United States of America, where I reside, the governor is the highest state official. When I was asked to serve on the Governor's Council and to pose for a photograph with him, I could not help remembering the text which one of my high-school classmates from Caribbean Union College, Trinidad, had written in my album. "The spider taketh hold with her hands, and is in kings' palaces."

Yes, spiders "may be found almost everywhere: on or near water, in or on the ground, from underground caves to the tops of mountains. In fact, salticid spiders have been taken as high as 22,000 feet on Mt. Everest. . . . Ballooning spiders have actually been collected from airplanes at an elevation of 5,000 feet. Some kinds of spiders live inside human habitations."[7] Probably this is the kind to which the Bible refers, that lives "in kings' palaces." But how do these spiders reach such heights? THEY USE WHAT THEY'VE GOT.

I am not aware of any structure more delicate and yet more complex than a spider's web. Some of the individual strands can barely be seen with the naked eye, but the spider knows how to use each strand. It produces a cocoon of silk within which its eggs are laid, and some spiders enclose extra silk padding before closing up the egg sac. "In some the outer covering is thin and meshy, in others quite tough, and in still others papery in texture."[8] The outer coverings may be of different consistencies. All do not have to have the same characteristics in order to be functional. Neither do all persons need to have the same qualifications in order to perform a task.

"One of the most interesting uses to which silk is put by some spiders is a 'parachute.' The spider climbs up high on a blade of grass, on a fence, or pole, and facing the wind stands on the tips of the tarse and tilts the abdomen upwards. From the spinnerets are emitted threads which are paid out as the air currents pull, until the bouyancy of the parachute is enough to support the spider, which releases its hold and is carried away in the breeze."[9]

No wonder spiders turn out to be so successful in getting around. They know how to USE WHAT THEY'VE GOT.

Never minimize what you've got. Recognize it for what it is. What you've got might be of critical importance. Follow the cause-and-effect relationship expressed in the next six lines:

> For the lack of a nail, the shoe was lost.
> For the lack of a shoe, the horse was lost.
> For the lack of a horse, the man was lost.
> For the lack of a man, the battle was lost.
> For the lack of a battle, the kingdom was lost.
> All for the lack of a horse-shoe nail.
>   —Author Unknown

Too often individuals tend to assess what they've got as insignificant or even valueless, because they think it does not measure up to what others are able to offer. But let us remember—

> Little drops of water
> Little grains of sand
> Make the mighty ocean
> And the pleasant land.
> —Author Unknown

Many individuals will not agree to be the stream if they can't be the river. They always want to be peaks—never valleys. They are not aware that valleys are part of the patterning. They always want to be doing what to them seems great. If a task is to be accomplished through team effort, the average person immediately begins to separate the roles of the participants into highest, higher, high; low, lower, lowest. Think of the last time you analyzed a situation in this fashion. If, however, that "lowest" team partner were to malfunction, the whole project might be a failure. The Go-getter does his best regardless of the classification of the task—be it great or small.

Let us look in on a team in a steroid laboratory. Its members are working with some radioactive material. Although the sample has been purchased from a reputable biochemical company and is labeled "pure," it is still necessary to run a purification test in order to verify that the sample meets the purity standard of this particular steroid laboratory. This task is performed by a research chemist. After the purification and solubility testing, a certain amount of radioactive material—in a specific concentration of saline—is injected into the subject.

As a research endocrinologist, my subjects were humans, and since we were using radioactive materials as tracers in order to test such factors as circulation and metabolic rate, the trace of radioactive substance had to be injected by a physician.[10] This particular team consisted of two chemists, a physician, and the subjects or clients.

Read carefully now and notice how every facet of this research—and therefore the work of every team member—is important. To obtain valid results, twenty-four-hour urine samples had to be accurately collected. We couldn't afford to have anyone participate in the research project as a team member who felt that his part was insignificant.

If one of the subjects had said, "I was not at home, so I couldn't save one portion of urine," or "I knew you wanted all the urine, so although I was not at home and had forgotten to take one of the treated containers with me, I saved the urine in another container and then poured it in with the portion I had already saved," the results would have been useless. While collecting the urine was a non-technical, routine part of the study, this aspect of the task was just as important as any other to the success of the project, since it was the urine that had to be analyzed. Being a team player is very important, because the success of the team depends on each individual's excellence. What one has to do is to make the best use of what he's got.

When the statement "USE WHAT YOU'VE GOT" is made, many will think of money or property or education. But if this chapter referred only to such advantages, this book might serve a limited purpose for most of my readers.

If we look at some of the important things in life available to most of us, we recognize that life is worth living. For example, in this chapter we have already considered the importance of performing small tasks well. If you have that ability, you are well on your way to becoming a Go-getter.

Now we will focus on three more valuable personal resources: courage, contact with God, and talents.

Courage

Most people have a certain measure of health and strength, yet some are constantly complainers. Many have simple, acute illnesses and feel helpless, while others have chronic diseases and yet are of service.

Meg Casey is said to be the longest surviving victim of a rare, deadly malady called progeria. This malady, which turns children into old people, usually kills its victims by the time they reach adolescence. But Meg has passed the quarter-of-a-century mark. Not many victims are known. In fact, fewer than 100 cases have been reported worldwide since 1886, when a British doctor, Jonathan Hutchinson, described the syndrome. This disorder—called the Hutchinson-Gilford progeria syndrome—stunts growth, disintegrates bones and muscles, and causes baldness and bulging eyes.

Although Meg suffers from this disorder, she does not sit around feeling sorry for herself. She recently read about younger progeriacs who were being told they would die soon, and she also read that a meeting was being planned at Disney World in Florida for young progeriacs. She attended that meeting as living proof that they could make much use of the life they've got.

Meg learned as much as she could from Yale-New Haven geneticists, and now she encourages not only progeriacs but disabled persons. Meg is a real Go-getter. She writes newspaper articles, appears on television, and runs a counseling center for the disabled. She has the courage to make life worthwhile for herself, and she is using it to the fullest as she helps others.[11]

Meg has the courage to use her inner strength—and

her love for others. She doesn't have height and beauty, but she doesn't sit around wishing for what is not. She uses what she has. Are You "Using What You've Got?"

Until recently, Meg was virtually unknown, but almost everyone has heard of Franklin D. Roosevelt. On a gloomy spring day in March 1933, FDR took the oath of office as the thirty-second President of the United States. This was the tail end of the Great Depression, so "he set about restoring confidence by acting confidently himself, and in an amazingly short time a surge of optimism spread throughout most of the American people."[12]

Without untold courage, FDR would never have attempted—much less succeeded at—becoming President of the United States. You see, in the 1920s Franklin D. Roosevelt became a victim of poliomyelitis. But he did not sit in a wheelchair throwing all of his talents away. He gave account for what he had, not for what he did not have. FDR was a real Go-getter. He knew that "the Go-getter works till he reaps what he sows for."

"To stand back and look at the man as a whole, against the backdrop of his people and his times, is to see lineaments of greatness—courage, joyousness, responsiveness, vitality, faith, and above all, concern for his fellow man."[13] Roosevelt "believed in doing good, and in showing people how to do good. By 'good' he meant the Ten Commandments and the Golden Rule."[14]

No matter what your circumstances of life, courage will bring you closer to your goal. Always remember to focus on the potential you have instead of using your energy to worry about what you do not have.

Contact With God

Another very important asset you possess is that of contact—contact with God. Earlier in this volume I mentioned that my mother would "pray me through" examinations. She had that contact with God. And guess what? I have it—and it is also available to you!

Early one summer my husband, our year-old son, and I were living in student housing at Atlantic Union College (AUC). We were both students, so when our semester grades arrived in one envelope addressed to both of us, I opened it even though my husband was not at home. We had the same teacher in one course, so when it was convenient we would study together or review each other before an examination. But it was always convenient for us to check our grades with each other, and they were usually about the same. For two working people with a young child, B's at AUC were good grades.

But this particular day when the final grade for the entire course arrived, my husband's grade was a B + and my grade was a C +. I knew it had to be a mistake—not that his grade should be lower but that mine should be higher! Of course, to me that was really no problem. I would just go to the teacher and explain away the mistake.

The teacher was very understanding. He showed me the grade book for the semester, and I saw where the reader had entered a zero (or naught) when I had actually received 100 percent on a particular test. I explained this to the teacher, who said, "Well, it could be that she thought you never took the test, or it could be that she never received the test. However," he continued, "if you can bring me your graded examination as proof, I will change your grade. But mind you," he added, "I have never had to do this in all my years of teaching."

I told him that would be fine and then left, saying to myself, "That's no problem. I will just go to my desk, get all my examinations, and take them to him. He can have all the proof he needs."

Well, easier said than done. The student apartments

were small, so every item had to be kept in its place. I
went directly to my desk and started to pull out test after
test. They were not filed—my returned examinations
were just placed in the drawer. Without any trouble, I
found all my exams for that course—except one. I abso-
lutely could not find the one for which I had claimed a 100
percent grade. I now hurriedly emptied the entire
drawer, scrambling my way even through examinations
from other courses—but to no avail.

I called my babysitter, who lived in an adjacent apart-
ment, explained my plight, and asked her to assist me.
Displaying a calm spirit now, probably because of her
supporting presence, I looked again at every examination. I found all of my husband's just as the teacher had
them in his record book. And I found all of mine also—
just as the teacher had them in his record book. Yes—the
reader had entered a zero because she seemed to have no
examination for me. And as confirmation, I could not find
the corrected examination.

Now I was becoming desperate. The grade was no
longer important. My reputation for honesty was at
stake. I said to my babysitter, "Let us kneel and ask God
to help us find this exam." We both prayed, and then we
renewed our search. But there was a difference. Now it
was as if—since we had involved God—we were going to
have to be very careful and do a really good job of searching, because God often uses people to help answer their
own prayers.

We went through every examination v-e-r-y c-a-r-e-f-
u-l-l-y—and found nothing. As we knelt to pray a second
time, a sudden gust of wind rushed through an open win-
dow. The wind scattered my loose papers all over the
room, separating them just enough for me to see that my
missing exam and my husband's had adhered so closely
together that they seemed as one.

We had made contact with God, and this time He used a mighty rushing wind to help me instead of a still small voice.[15] God will do His part for us, and if we are not in contact with Him, let us establish that contact today. He knows what is best for us, so if He seems to say No to one of our requests—and we *truly* love Him—we will accept His will for us.

The Talent

An understanding person usually has many friends. Understanding is a characteristic that can be developed and is a rewarding talent.

You undoubtedly have read the parable of the talents. "The kingdom of heaven is as a man travelling into a far country, who called his own servants, and delivered unto them his goods. And unto one he gave five talents, to another two, and to another one; to every man according to his several ability."[16]

Because some people ably perform several tasks, you should not think of yourself as worthless because you can perform only one task well. People possess different abilities, and it is doing your best with what you've got that matters most. The parable says that the two servants with five and two talents doubled theirs, but the servant that had one talent hid it.

If you do not have education, money, or property to share, but you do have understanding, that is a talent most would love to possess. The master called the servant who hid his talent a wicked and slothful servant and told him that because he had not used the talent, it would be given to the one who had ten talents. If you don't use what you've got, you'll lose what you've got.

I have a friend—a former classmate. I'll call him "C. J." When he arrived at boarding school, he got lost in the

crowd. He was average at many endeavors—as most of us
are. He did not display his real talent because that talent,
he thought, lacked status for a young man in boarding
school.

Then his special talent was revealed. He was able to
repair shoes. He could put new soles on shoes, he could
repair heels, he could mend uppers—he could make a pair
of shoes as good as new, for half the price. C. J. became
very popular on the campus. Everyone knew him. When
an election was held for any position in which C. J. was
interested, he won it because he was so well known. He
still works for the Seventh-day Adventist denomination
today, and his popularity has not waned. Talents have a
way of multiplying, if you "Use What You've Got."

Dr. Adlai Esteb once shared an incident in the life of
Dwight L. Moody which led me to believe that Moody had
little with which to work. Esteb said that Moody heard
Henry Varley, a preacher from England, say, "The world
has yet to see what God can do through a man wholly
dedicated to Him." Moody put his head down in his hand
and said, "Oh, God—I will be that man!" Thereafter
Moody became a dedicated man.

Later, in one of Moody's meetings, a very distinguished
gentleman went up to Moody after the meeting and said,
"Mr. Moody, I counted eleven mistakes of grammar in
your speech tonight. A man who is speaking to vast audiences ought to be more careful with his diction." Moody
felt a lump in his throat, and he said, "I am sorry, sir. I
didn't have very much schooling. I never got beyond the
eighth grade. I don't know very much grammar, but I am
using all that I have to the glory of God. Sir, what are you
doing with yours?"

Whatever your talent may be, do not hide it. Develop it
to the best of your ability. Maximize your potential by
recognizing the importance of accepting small tasks and

performing them well. Have courage like that of Meg Casey and the late President Roosevelt. Establish and retain contact with God. And multiply what you've got as C. J. did.

A quadriplegic once said, "My limbs might be gone but not my brains." Others who had limbs were able to assist him physically, while he assisted them in other ways. He decided to make use of what he had instead of worrying about what he did not have.

IF was not part of his vocabulary, and it does not have to be part of yours. We will consider this topic in our next chapter.

IF Is Not Part of Your Vocabulary

"Seest thou a man diligent in his business? he shall stand before kings; he shall not stand before mean men."[17]

This text refers to both men and women. It refers to the attitudes people have toward life and the results that inevitably follow. Diligence presumes involvement in worthwhile activities—activities considered important by the person pursuing them. For the Go-getter, diligence is part of the upward climb—part of the positive forward motion toward success. How diligent are you about what you do? With a positive attitude you will move in the right direction.

This chapter explains how to handle situations positively. And it suggests how to avoid the following IFs:

> The Circumstantial IF
> The Dependent IF
> The Negative and Positive IF
> The Opaque IF

The Circumstantial IF

Too often individuals create barriers for themselves because of a negative attitude. They need excuses not to succeed, so they develop a litany—the first stanza of which reveals the stance of the coward and pleads for *another tool*. "IF only I had the Prince's sword, I would be able to perform mighty feats." Others might say, "IF only I had transportation, I would visit the sick or the prisoners and take some literature and a word of cheer—but I don't have a car." They cannot accept the small inconvenience of using public transportation.

The second stanza focuses on *another place*. "IF I were in another country, another state, another school, I would be able to accomplish my purpose or fulfill my goal. There they would appreciate me more, and there would be more opportunities." Looking for "another place" is a serious mistake which too many people make. They look to other pastures which—while at some distance—seem greener. The other fellow's territory seems to have a little more potential for growth. "IF I can just get transferred to another church, another school, another company, my problems will be over."

Most people apply for and get jobs with an organization. But then it is up to them to turn those jobs into positions! Don't be running around looking for something better—instead, better the something that you have.

The third stanza wishes for *another time*. "IF it were only some other time. I just can't do it now. Probably I can perform that task tomorrow, but not today." But remember that when "tomorrow" arrives it will be "today" again. These complainers all utilize the Circumstantial IF and fail. "Procrastination is the thief of time." Do not succumb to the fallacy of "another time." "On the sands of hesitation lie the bones of countless millions who at dawn of victory lay down to rest, and resting, died."

Go-getters do not create barriers for themselves, and *IF* is not part of their vocabulary. They do not seek another tool, another place, or another time. "The Go-getter fixes a goal and resolves when he sets it, / The way to the prize is to go till he gets it."

You may have read the account of how John Bunyan wrote *Pilgrim's Progress* while languishing for twelve years in the prison of Bedford Castle. He did not say "IF only I had some stationery on which to write, I would write a book."

Every day he was brought a utensil containing milk, and around the cover was a small piece of brown wrapping paper. He saw something that he could use in that little piece of brown wrapping paper. Each day he saved the pieces of paper, and eventually he had saved enough paper to write a good portion of the book *Pilgrim's Progress*. That book is among the most widely circulated books ever written.

John Bunyan did not create any barriers. Instead he used what he had and succeeded. He ignored the Circumstantial IF, and he succeeded.

The Dependent IF

Some people do not create barriers, but they worry so much about barriers that they forget to exercise trust in God. In fact, they never fully realize just how destructive worry is. Worry truly plays havoc with one's life. It ruins digestion, causes stomach ulcers, interferes with sleep, and decreases sound judgment. But examples are available to us of people who, instead of worrying, exercised trust in God.

Case in point: Jesus is on a mission of restoration, and the crowd is following Him to see what miracles He will perform. Speculation is rife—what miracles will He perform today? Opinions are divided. Arguments and excited discussions can be heard. Some declare that He can work miracles—others say He is bound to fail.

In the crowd are beggars with trembling lips, those with sightless eyes that stare, and those who tap with sticks on the pavement. But also in the crowd is another—having no trembling lips or staring eyes, but whose face is streaked with pain. For twelve years she has suffered. She has sought and paid for all the medical help available, but her case still seems incurable. She has heard of Jesus of Nazareth and what He has done for others. A thought strikes her—a daring, terrifying idea perhaps, but worth trying.

She does not stop at "IF only I could get through the crowd," or "IF only I could get near Him," or "IF only I could touch Him." No, IF is not part of her vocabulary. She decides that she must touch Jesus. She has faith that a touch will mean healing for her. She eases her way through the crowd, but the closer she gets to Jesus, the more people get in her way.

It would be so easy for her to say, "I have done my best. No one can say I didn't try," and then give up. But that is not her way of dealing with barriers. She is a Go-getter, and getting what she has come for is a matter of life and death. In pain and near exhaustion she presses through the crowd. She can see Him now. She only needs to reach Him. Just a few more feet! She must touch Him. Now she is desperate. She will not lose this opportunity. He is coming in her direction. At last—He is passing. She reaches out her hand and barely touches His robe.

She has touched the hem of Jesus' garment, and even amidst the crushing crowd, she feels His healing power within her veins and arteries and lungs and muscles. Then—she retreats into the crowd. But Jesus knows that someone has drawn healing power from Him, and when His gaze and the woman's have met, and they have exchanged kind words, Jesus says, "Daughter, thy faith hath made thee whole."[18]

Faith is the victory that overcomes the world. Let us lay hold on faith and not allow negative IF statements to hinder us from performing the tasks with which we have been entrusted.

This sick woman had set a goal, and because of her circumstances, she could have fallen back on the "Dependent IF" and said, "IF Jesus would just pass my way," or "IF the church elders would only help me get through that crowd," or "IF the young people would only 'run interference' for me so that I wouldn't have to fight the crowds, then I might see Jesus and be healed." There were so many plausible excuses she could have made. But IF was not part of her vocabulary, and IF should not be a part of *your* vocabulary!

The Negative and Positive IF

With a positive attitude toward the accomplishment of your task, you are well on your way to success. No clear line of demarcation exists between benefits and barriers. In fact, sometimes they overlap, and at other times one person's barrier might be another's benefit. This means that not only are circumstances important, but also one's perception of them.

Peter and John were rich men and poor men simultaneously. How could that be? "Now Peter and John went up together into the temple at the hour of prayer, being the ninth hour. And a certain man lame from his mother's womb was carried, whom they laid daily at the gate of the temple which is called Beautiful, to ask alms of them that entered into the temple; who seeing Peter and John about to go into the temple asked an alms. And Peter, fastening his eyes upon him with John, said, Look on us. And he gave heed unto them, expecting to receive something of them. Then Peter said, Silver and gold have

I none; but such as I have give I thee; In the name of Jesus
Christ of Nazareth rise up and walk."[19]

As the people saw the healed man leaping and praising
God, they were filled with amazement. And Peter said,
"Ye men of Israel, why marvel ye at this?" He told them
that God had glorified His Son Jesus.

Note the attitude displayed by Peter and John—how
they perceived themselves. They were positive about being rich instead of negative about being poor. When
asked for alms, Peter didn't say, "IF I had money, I would
be happy to help you." He simply explained the circumstances. "Silver and gold have I none; but such as I have
give I thee: In the name of Jesus Christ of Nazareth"—
note to whom the credit went—"rise up and walk." They
were rich because Christ lived in them and used them.

Esther was a Bible character whose position was dangerous because of prevailing circumstances but who perceived that position as full of potential benefit to her people. She did not tell Mordecai, "IF only I could find a way
to help my people, so that they will not be put to death, I
would!" She made a way. She said, "I will go in unto the
king, which is not according to the law: and if I perish, I
perish."[20]

Esther was willing to take the risk and accept responsibility for her actions. Are we willing to do the same? With
every opportunity comes a responsibility. Some are anx-
ious for opportunities but are not willing to accept the
responsibilities that go with them. Being diligent in business means recognizing opportunities and responsibilities as twins.

The Opaque IF

Being diligent in business also means becoming prepared to embrace fleeting opportunities when they

arise—and thus attain success. Being diligent means recognizing the importance of the relationship between subgoals and main goals. Any position which is less than best is not a permanent position but is only a stepping-stone—a subgoal. And your horizons change, because a horizon is nothing but the limit to sight. So what's your limit?

"One day in 1885 a crowd of people gathered in a Chicago street for the inauguration of a very strange building—in fact a modern miracle: it was a house twelve stories high, the first of its kind. The people of Chicago had watched it grow taller and taller, and someone called it a 'skyscraper,' and the name stuck."[21]

Now in New York City stands the World Trade Center. In Chicago stands the Sears Tower. Both of these structures are over 100 stories high. How high are your sights?

When Henry Bessemer, at the age of seventeen, began his inventions, he did not start out with the idea of one day becoming the "Father of the Skyscraper." In fact, in 1830 his parents had recently moved to London from a country village, and Henry felt lost. "A new world seemed open to me. The metropolis with its thousands of vehicles and pedestrians, its gorgeous shops and stately buildings . . . overwhelmed me with wonder and astonishment. And yet there was one thing strange to me, and sadly wanting. I felt that I was alone; no one knew me."[22] This feeling of loneliness, coupled with Henry's feelings of inferiority to other young men, was one of the mainsprings which drove his ambition. Before long he would set out to conquer London.

Bessemer did not say, "I am so young. IF I were even twenty-one I could branch out and make a name for myself." No, he began with an invention which was adopted by his government and saved it a lot of money, but made no money for himself. But, pleased that he had been able to serve, he continued with other inventions. Bessemer conquered not only London but the "whole world and the Seven Seas."[23]

You too can be successful. Many different levels of success exist. IF ONLY is no substitute for success. Often people become discouraged with themselves and their attainments. They attempt to make unequal comparisons between their own accomplishments and those of others without knowing how the circumstances might have been different. I have only two offspring—a son and a daughter—and each of them graduated from college at an earlier age than I graduated from high school.

Illness in your immediate family, or starting a family, may have forced some of you to postpone your education. Others of you may have had your schooling interrupted by war. Still others may have had no role models, and therefore did not understand the importance of higher education. Or perhaps no school was located in your area where you could obtain higher education. And there may be a hundred and one other reasons.

But suppose that now you *do* have an opportunity for more education. By comparing yourself with someone your own age who already has a higher education—who might even be your teacher if you return to school—you could become discouraged and abandon your plans. But this would be a great mistake.

Not knowing the circumstances under which that other person succeeded, you could make an unfavorable comparison and lose the opportunity to develop your own maximum potential. You might even unknowingly be comparing your worst features with their best.

Do not let that happen to you. I would be thoroughly disappointed if—after you have read this far—you did not go right out and find a way to arrive at whatever goal you have been considering all these years—be it academic or nonacademic. "Do not wait for an opening; make one for yourselves."[24]

Some time ago one of my professors told his class that Thomas Edison once explained his own creative accomplishments by saying, "Genius is one percent inspiration and ninety-nine percent perspiration." Persistence and dedication are threads in the same fabric.

Making a way for yourself is not easy. Even when someone is there to assist you, achieving your goal may present some difficulty. You must therefore be goal oriented and goal directed and make a habit of performing small tasks well. Because "actions repeated form habits, habits form character."[25] "Make a success of the present duty."[26] But success is an uphill pathway. And as you pursue your goals, you will find obstacles. One quotation I have used as a guiding light since high school says that "when a man, a real man, has set a goal, it is better for his opponent to endeavor to block the great Mississippi with straw than to try to stop him." You might need to remove barriers, but "the breaking down of one barrier will give greater ability and courage to go forward. Press with determination in the right direction, and circumstances will be your helpers, not your hindrances."[27] Often we set our sights too low. We fail to understand that if we aim for the stars, we will at least reach the trees.

Among the many positions I held as I attempted to finance my education was one which involved screening applicants for various jobs. Often as I analyzed an applicant's educational record, I noted the statement "Registered at College X" or "Attended College Y." Attending an educational institution and not graduating is not a disgrace, but since "almost" is usually not enough, why not attempt to complete what you have begun?

Be the master of your fate. With Jesus as your Guide, you may "pull out all the stops and go till you get what you are going for." Remember that you are not the only one who may have procrastinated in completing some project. Some people equate failure in one project with failure in life. But let me give you some encouragement. While I was studying toward my doctor's degree at Harvard University, I still took some time out to speak at camp meetings and at various churches. During that time many church members and pastors suggested that I write at least a small volume, so that more people would benefit from my presentations. I agreed that it was a good idea, and for a few years I promised that I would. But I never set a deadline. Then about seven years ago, I wrote the first chapter under a different title, and it was destroyed in a fire. Yet here I am again after seven years. If I can do it, so can you.

You need to be careful about what you do and don't do, because you might be someone's model in your church, your school, your community. Often those who stagnate might be the yardstick for many others. *You* might be the yardstick—so how about making that move today?

You think IF can be a hindrance? Wait until you read what NEVER can do!

Never Is Not a Word

"I can do all things through Christ which strengtheneth me."[28]

When Go-getters accept congratulations for their accomplishments, they do so with the full acknowledgment that it is only through Christ that all things are possible. They are aware that success in any area of life is determined by how much God works through them and not by how much they can do by themselves.

Go-getters also recognize that even the longest journey toward success begins with just one step—and that the first step is nearest to them. So to climb to the high peak of their goal, they must "Begin Where They Are." But how are they going to reach that peak? By some mechanical device? By foot? How are they going to pursue that academic goal? By working eight hours a day? By waiting to see if a scholarship comes their way? You know the answer—they should "Use What They've Got." They should pay no attention to what others have or to how comfortable their journey might seem. Go-getters might even be tempted to begrudge others their success, citing supposed advantages. And then they could be tempted to say, "IF only I had what they've got." But IF is not part of a Go-getter's vocabulary.

When people visualize the distance to their goal, they are sometimes tempted to feel they will never reach it. But goals are attained through incremental steps, and for those who take those steps, "*Never* Is Not a Word." You may not reach your goal today, but the pursuit is all-important. And arriving at subgoals is one mechanism for reaching goals. Always remember, "The Go-getter works till he reaps what he sows for."

In this chapter we will first consider a case study in success. Then we will focus on barriers—perceived as well as created barriers—and how to deal with them.

Success—A Case Study

I have not known him well enough or long enough to refer to him as my friend, but we have interacted professionally. If anyone has acceptable reason to be nonfunctional, it is this man. He was born without any arms.

As director for the ("International Year for the Disabled") program at Atlantic Union College, I invited Dr. Wilke to be the guest speaker. I selected the most sensitive and caring people I knew of to work with him, and my secretary, Mrs. Marilyn Spangler, volunteered to assist him. Thus Dr. Wilke would not have to explain to several people at different times what his immediate needs were. I asked my husband to meet Dr. Wilke at the airport. I wanted to be certain someone sensitive, yet strong and willing would be on hand to help care for the needs of our guest.

How surprised I was! Where others would have used their hands, Dr. Wilke used his feet. Where others would have used their fingers, he used his toes. As Dr. Wilke spoke to the congregation, he not only reached into his pocket for a notepad, but he turned the pages of the Bible with his toes—like a person with no handicap. Later, in conversation with him at the dining table, he told me that his parents expected him to do everything his brothers did, so he had to find alternate ways.

It is our duty to find alternate ways to achieve success. Instead of saying, "I will NEVER be able to accomplish such a task," find a way—or make one. Because for a Go-getter, "*Never* Is Not a Word."

Too often individuals tend to perceive barriers to success that are not even present, or worse yet, they create barriers.

Perceived Barriers

Many activities occur in the world, some of which concern all of us, and all of which concern some of us. Most of us, however, react to those happenings which we think may either create circumstances beneficial to us or create barriers for us.

Dr. Wilke's barrier was permanent—it was genetic. He could not remove it, so he very ably circumvented it. Most people encounter temporary barriers. Some give up, but others overcome by using detours. At times in the pursuit of success so many barriers appear that the only way to proceed may be to select and overcome them one at a time.

Created Barriers

The most dangerous barriers are the ones we create for ourselves, such as fear and discouragement.

Let us look at fear for a moment. You have probably heard of the word *phobia*. This word is defined as an "intense and overwhelming fear of something which, as the phobic person realizes, actually poses no major threat.

The most common phobias include acrophobia (fear of
high places), claustrophobia (fear of close places),
agoraphobia (fear of open places), and ophidiaphobia
(fear of snakes). But people can develop phobias for almost anything: germs, fire, blood, water, cats, dogs, bees,
whatever."[29]

Another fear for people pursuing a goal is fear of failure. Fear of failure has paralyzed many individuals, especially when family or friends display a negative attitude
or themselves express the fear of failure. But remember,
you are in charge. Shift your energies away from dwelling on failure and use them to concentrate on success.
Have you ever heard of persons who fail in a task before
they have even begun? One writer says, "Nothing fails
like failure." Another writer says, "Success is failure
turned inside out."

The account that I will now share with you is one of a
crisis situation that hung in the balance for approxi-
mately three weeks. The fear-of-failure barrier was created for me by many well-wishers, but I would not succumb. I would not give up because for a Go-getter, "*Never*
Is Not a Word."

My course work was completed, my proposal had been
accepted, my research was done, my thesis was submit-
ted; and now all that remained was my defense of my thesis. My committee of readers consisted of a sociologist, a
psychologist, and a psychiatrist. The date for the defense
of the thesis had been set, but the sociologist—the major
advisor—became ill. A second date was set, but the psychologist was near death after being almost electrocuted
on his farm after a storm. Now only a week remained for
me to defend my thesis if the results were to be processed
in time for graduation.

As the first two scheduled defense dates passed, my
mother was very ill, but then improved—though she was

yet hospitalized. However, she suddenly worsened and died. Under these difficult circumstances, I was compelled to defend my thesis or wait another year to graduate. And the position I hoped to fill after graduation required a doctoral degree, and that post could not remain unfilled for a year.

Condolences and suggestions poured in. "Wait until after the funeral—you will be calm then." "Take your exam before the funeral—you will be too grieved immediately afterward and will not be able to concentrate." "You will never be able to pass if you try to do it right now."

The way may be dark. You may feel bewildered. Suggestions may be forthcoming and very helpful. But you must make your own decisions. My mother had died, but she had acted on what the wise man Solomon once said: "Train up a child in the way he should go."[30] She had taught me how to make contact with heaven. And when the answer came in the form of the text "I can do all things through Christ which strengtheneth me," I knew I was being told to go and take my examination.

After a grueling oral examination, the committee sent me to a room to wait alone for the results. What they did not know is that I had a Friend with me all through the examination, and He was now in the room with me. Jesus is an ever-present help in time of need. He saw me through, and He will do the same for you. He who rules the universe knows the end from the beginning and will provide light at the end of the tunnel if we will but trust Him. We need fear only if we forget how God has led us in the past.

Another devastating fear is fear of the unknown. This is another barrier people sometimes create for themselves. However, if no one ever walked off the beaten path, no new paths would be created. If all people thought alike, it would be as if no one had a thought. In order to be an authority and not an echo, people must reach out into the unknown. Go-getters must do more than reflect other men's thoughts. Go-getters must be creative. They must be innovative. They must contribute new ideas. They must be willing both to create and to accept change.

In the early days of the Seventh-day Adventist denomination, it was called a "movement." One outstanding literature evangelist—Elder A. R. Haig—would say, "This is a movement—and if we do not move with the movement, the movement will move and leave us behind." Movement suggests change, and change involves moving into the unknown. Go-getters cannot afford to fear the unknown, because they must learn to create new knowledge by research and discovery. A ship in port is safe, but that is not what ships are made for. They must venture into uncharted waters.

Yet another barrier people often create for themselves is the fear of success. Few people are aware of the fear of success.

I was not aware that fear of success was so extensive until about ten years ago when I conducted a class on social mobility and read the papers my students had written.

Let me explain social mobility. This is any movement in the social arena from one social status to another. Sometimes such a movement is horizontal—a person remains on the same level. For example, a change in job but not in salary would be horizontal mobility. Or the movement might be vertical, in which a person begins to climb the ladder of success. Such job changes are usually accompanied by salary increases and by promotion to a higher position in the organization.

As I read the students' papers, I recognized that many were fearful about graduating from college—fearful of the added responsibilities this educational preparation would bring. One elementary-school teacher would be expected to become the principal. A worker in a particular organization would have to leave the comforts of the routine to learn about other areas in the organization. Another senior expressed anxiety about being expected to know everything in her educational field.

Professionals who offer educational assistance and meet with rejection need to understand the underlying reasons. Some young people say, "I will *never* go to college." Others say, "I will *never* become a physician. Let somebody else take the responsibility." This is all part of the fear-of-success syndrome and is a barrier to success that could be overcome. For the Go-getter, "*Never* Is Not a Word."

One more barrier that blocks the path to success for many is the barrier of discouragement.

> There's many an auto equipped with a starter
> That starts up the hill like the charge of a tartar,
> But soon it is found, it has also a stopper—

Is that stopper the barrier of discouragement? Success is the combination of preparation and opportunity—and preparation is not always pleasurable. In fact, it is often painful. Painful in terms of sacrifices that must be made—sacrifices of time, of energy, of finances. But too many individuals have given up trying when they unknowingly were on the verge of triumph. They have said, "I will *never* make it." Do not join them.

Remember that you are a Go-getter, and for Go-getters, "*Never* Is Not a Word." Don't be discouraged. Even a clock that does not work shows the correct time twice a day. Think positive thoughts. Have you ever heard of anyone sharpening a razor on velvet? Today there are many unsuccessful people with great talents. The reason for their failure is that they gave up *yesterday*. One of the most successful barriers to success is the barrier of discouragement.

Barrier Removal

As we discuss barrier removal, let us be certain we agree that there are positive as well as negative barriers. Better far to erect a barrier at the top of the hill around the school than to place an ambulance down in the valley. But negative barriers can be broken down, whether they be fear of failure, fear of the unknown, fear of success, or even the barrier of discouragement. The process for their removal is similar:

1. Have a positive mental attitude.
2. Effect change gradually in the circumstance or situation.
3. Remember that anyone can react positively to the positive. You are special when you can react positively to the negative.
4. Know that all things are possible if you have trust in God.
5. In the pursuit of true success, "*Never* Is Not a Word."

Overcoming barriers takes knowledge, skill, and willpower—which includes exercising self-control. Many people fail because they expect immediate results. Overcoming barriers takes knowledge. Many people fail because they have not clearly defined their goals. Success has passed them by while they were still searching for it. Success is relative and is dependent on time and space. Likewise, how a weed is seen is relative. What is identified as a weed in one setting might in another setting be termed a pretty flower. In attempting to remove barriers, you may need to do some transplanting of yourself.

Overcoming barriers takes skill. If a seed is planted in the right kind of soil and is nurtured, it will grow. And while a farmer or a botanist has not given that seed life, he can determine the direction the plant will grow. If he restricts the light to a narrow beam of sunlight which "calls" the plant upward, it will grow thin and fragile. He has skill and may use it to condition the environment. These attributes—willpower, knowledge, and skill—are necessary for survival. If you do not possess them, develop them. Remember, "Diamonds are only chunks of coal—that stuck to their job."

> A diamond in the rough
> Is a diamond sure enough.
> For before it ever sparkled
> It was made of diamond stuff.
> But someone had to find it
> Or it never would be found,
> And someone had to grind it
> Or it never would be ground.
> But when it is found,
> And when it is ground,
> And when it is burnished bright,
> That diamond everlastingly
> Just shines forth its light.*

As a Go-getter, you have set your goal. As a Go-getter, you are pursuing your goal. And as a Go-getter, you will reach your goal. Because you will stick to your job, you will remove barriers, and you will retain a positive mental attitude, because for you, *"Never* Is Not a Word."

---

* Taught to the children of the St. Johns, Antigua, Seventh-day Adventist Elementary School by the late Pastor J. T. Carrington of the Caribbean Union.

As a Go-getter, you will reach your goal because you discard the barriers of fear which can drain your energies. As a Go-getter, you will reach your goal because you have faith in God and belief in yourself. I am told that when Henry Ford made his first car, he did not include any reverse gear. How about you? Will it be forward all the way?

Success is not measured only by the position held, but by the obstacles surmounted and the barriers removed. Success is like a ratio. It is a measurement of what you are, against what you might have been. Expect the best from yourself. *Exact* the best from yourself and know that "Your Best Is Enough."

Your Best Is Enough

"His lord said unto him, Well done, thou good and faithful servant: thou hast been faithful over a few things, I will make thee ruler over many things: enter thou into the joy of thy lord."[31]

You have been faithful, God says. You have recognized your responsibilities. You have lived up to My expectations. You have performed your duties well in My absence. You have proved yourself worthy of My confidence and trust. I will increase your status and improve your wages. You have been faithful over a few things. I will make you ruler over many things.

My interpretation of the above words is "Your Best Is Enough." Such compliments are not often heard. But when received, they are much appreciated.

One potential problem I must quickly bring to light is the possibility of regression. You see, there is a lot of room at the top, I am told, but there is no place to sit. Once you have arrived, you are expected to continue functioning with the same efficiency that got you there. Success is transitory and cannot be maintained if growth is halted.

Let us agree that "Your Best Is Enough." Then the larger question is, How do you know that you are at your best? You have become an excellent evaluator when you can determine that you have done your best. Knowing that you have done your best means that you understand the extent of your abilities, that you have observed the various steps included in your pursuit, and that you have accomplished your goals.

Another way to measure whether you are at your best is to determine whether you are happy and content in what you do. Of course the perception of happiness and contentment varies among individuals. A few precise questions might be necessary to help you in your evaluation. Let us put this evaluation in the context of a job situation:

1. Do you want to go to work?
2. Do you report for work, but you really do not want to go?
3. Do you report for work late?
4. Do you absent yourself from work as much as possible?
5. Do you report for work a few minutes early, or are you always barely on time?

Of course, *your* best does not have to be the same as someone else's. Your best is fulfilling what *you* set out to accomplish. Completing a task is a learning process. And in completing that task you learn more about yourself and your abilities. You may decide to keep growing in the same direction, or you may use your new know-how to go in another direction. Remember that we are talking about *you* and *your* fulfillment—*your* happiness. So whenever you decide that you are happy, content, and fulfilled in what you are doing, *that is your best*. And "Your Best Is Enough."

Your best should be the highest possible level you can attain in your particular area. It should not be mediocre.

Go-getters have a passion for excellence. You should not be content even to be the big fish in the little pond. In an effort to be your best, you may need to test yourself by aiming even higher than that which you can easily achieve. You must keep on stretching, even if it may seem to you that success seems to elude your grasp each time you reach a point at which you say, "This is it—I am going to succeed this time." The standard you set may seem to recede further as you advance toward it.

When you do not succeed at first, striving seems all the more challenging. Don't forget that one energetic attempt is worth a thousand aspirations. Becoming the best of whatever you are is not the results of a childlike fantasy. A clear distinction exists between fantasizing that success will miraculously come your way—and putting forth every effort to be the best of whatever you are. So before you can be safe in saying, "Your Best Is Enough," you must be sure *you are doing your best*.

This chapter will explore the meaning of being your best in three dimensions: educational preparation, health habits, and service to God and your fellowman. To be able to contribute your best, you must be educated to the height of your capabilities, you must develop a life-style which promotes health and prevents illness, and you must have love for God and man.

Educational Preparation—Your Best

"If any of you lack wisdom, let him ask God, that giveth to all men liberally, and upbraideth not."[32]

True education has to do with development of the whole person. Educational preparation begins in the home and continues throughout life. "Home is the first and most important school for the soul. It is there that every human being receives his most influential training, his best or his worst, for it is there that he imbibes those principles of conduct which endure through maturity and cease only with death."[33]

The basic training which people receive at home largely determines whether they will attain their highest goals.

A lifetime of bacteriological research had prepared Alexander Fleming to recognize the significance of a bit of fluff which had blown into a culture dish and stopped the growth of bacteria there. Something in the fluff, he reasoned, prevented this growth, and in publishing his observations, he noted that whatever was in the fluff could have usefulness in treating infections. When he experimented on people with infections, the substance sometimes cleared the infections miraculously and at other times did nothing. If the mysterious germ-inhibiting factor could be extracted and purified, it was clearly destined to be a powerful, lifesaving drug.

But according to Fleming's biographer, Andre Maurois, although Fleming continued to maintain cultures of his peculiar penicillium substance for the next twelve years, he could not convince his superiors of the attention this research deserved.[34]

According to Maurois, Fleming was particularly handicapped by an almost complete inability to express himself and confide his feelings to anyone. Fleming had grown up surrounded by bright older brothers, and although he was unable to enter into any of their conversations, he would listen—and from listening he had the satisfaction of learning.

Fleming was aware of his limitations in speech, which had developed as a result of the silent life he had lived as a child. But he did his best by publishing his observations. Later a biochemist came across Fleming's original paper by chance. Impressed, and believing Fleming dead, he enlisted the help of two other chemists. Within a matter of months they had purified and synthesized the germ-killing substance in penicillium—penicillin.

People who do their best by using the talents they have (without worrying about those they do not have) will prove triumphant in the end. Though he was a great scientist, educated in bacteriology, Fleming could not convince his superiors that he needed more money and manpower. But he was also an excellent researcher: he observed, documented, analyzed, and eventually published. And because of his original paper, penicillin is available today. His best was enough. "Your Best Is Enough." If you are a researcher, an analyst, a writer, a public speaker, or a manager—that is wonderful. But you do not have to possess ten talents to be your best—some people have only one talent.

Alexander Fleming's story shows that early home experiences influence us all through life. The home is the greatest learning environment. It develops social skills and molds attitudes. Within it, children develop their self-image and their value system. And educational preparation is highly dependent on this value system.

The school is second only to the home in educational preparation. A school should be carefully chosen, because learning takes place in informal situations with peers as well as in formal settings with teachers. When parents and students have the opportunity to select an educational institution, they should choose one in which there are teachers who can serve as role models. The educational institution selected should also be in harmony with one's goals and philosophy. It should produce educationally prepared and emotionally mature graduates.

Until early adulthood, the mind is very impressionable. Therefore young people should not be forced into positions where they must frequently say No. And they should not be asked to be different from their associates.

My father, the late Aaron E. Fenton of Montserrat, West Indies, often told us as children that he was the figurative stick at the gate of the pen to keep his little animals in. He would explain that it was much easier to keep them in than to round them up and return them to the pen.

The depth of the foundation determines the height of the structure. Therefore the proper educational foundation needs to be well laid. Only when this has been done can people develop to their highest potential. And only then can they be ready to do their best and know that their best is enough.

Nothing is more unfortunate than to find Seventh-day Adventist men and women who are educated to meet the world's standards but who fail to reach God's standards. Thus we are counseled to teach the Word diligently to our children. "These words, which I command thee this day, shall be in thine heart: and thou shalt teach them diligently unto thy children."[35]

In Bible times, instruction in the ways of the Lord was not to be a hit-and-miss affair. Children were to be taught diligently in the *ways* of the Lord. To accomplish this, schools of the prophets were established. And Ellen G. White says that before this, the Lord Himself had directed the education of Israel.[36]

The schools of the prophets were founded by Samuel to provide for the moral and spiritual welfare of the youth and to promote the future prosperity of the nation. "Train up a child in the way he should go"[37]—because character is caught, not taught. In fact, Aristotle said, concerning Greek education, that it was not clear whether education was more concerned with intellect or with character.

When I talk about character, I refer to that complex set of habitual behavior forms and ethical traits which distinguishes one person or group from another—the pattern of behavior which serves to individualize a person.

These behavior patterns which form our characters stem from our wills, and *will* in psychology is the name given to a person's power to act purposefully.

A youngster in conversation with the captain of a ship asked the captain how long he had been sailing in a particularly treacherous river. "For twenty-five years, I have sailed up and down this river," the captain replied.

"Then you know every rock and sand bank so that you can avoid them."

"No, I don't have to know them. But I do know where the deep water is—all the way."

Go-getters know what they are going for and attempt to follow as direct a pathway as possible. So they prepare themselves to the fullest. When this is accomplished they are ready to make their contribution and are satisfied that their best is enough. Such a contribution, of course, demands a healthy body.

Health Habits

"Beloved, I wish above all things that thou mayest prosper and be in health."[38]

That people function at a higher level when they are well is unquestionable. Therefore Go-getters, who naturally want to be at their best in whatever they attempt, will do all they can to maintain both a healthy mind and body.

As recently as two decades ago, definitions such as "peace is the absence of war," or "health is the absence of disease," were still being voiced. The view now, however, is that health is far more than simply the absence of disease. Good health also demands that people be able to adequately perform their tasks as workers, family members, and community participants. And life-style is a significant determinant of overall health.

In the early 1950s, four psychologists conducted research on health and developed what is known as the Health Belief Model (HBM).[39] Later, other researchers drew wide attention to this model.[40]

The Health Belief Model contains the following elements:

1. *Perceived Susceptibility*. This means that people who have been exposed to diseases—unless they see themselves as being susceptible—will probably not take any action to seek health care.

2. *Perceived Severity*. Exposed individuals who think they are susceptible to the disease in question—unless they perceive the consequences as severe—may also not seek health care.

3. *Perceived Benefits and Perceived Barriers*. People should perceive that by eating well-balanced meals (preferably with a time lapse before going to sleep), by exercising (preferably walking two or three miles a day), and by getting the necessary sleep, they will probably live much longer and gain many benefits. The barriers for such a program are minimal. The program calls only for commitment.

Why is the HBM important to you? Because the way you relate to it may determine your health status and whether you are prepared to function at your best. By recognizing the importance of these perceptions, you will be able to analyze and therefore understand what is actually happening to you and why you are behaving as you do. Then you will undoubtedly make more intelligent decisions as to your health habits. You will see that perceiving a lack of susceptibility, for example, does not guarantee immunity.

"The heaviest burdens of illness in the United States today are related to aspects of individual behavior, especially long-term patterns of behavior often referred to as 'lifestyle.' "[41] This, of course, is also true in other countries.

"Research has confirmed that some behaviors are risk factors of disease. That means that people who engage in such behaviors are more likely to develop certain types of illnesses than people who do not. Perhaps the most widely known association of this type is that of cigarette smoking as a risk factor of lung cancer. . . . Known behavioral risk factors include not only cigarette smoking, but excessive consumption of alcoholic beverages, use of illicit' drugs, certain dietary habits, insufficient exercise, reckless driving, nonadherence with sound medication regimens and maladaptive responses to social pressures."[42]

People interested in being effective will need to avoid behaviors which create disease risk factors. Go-getters will doubtless want to go a step further and assist others in this avoidance. Do not be discouraged, however, if you do not see behavior changes immediately. Many people find it extremely difficult to change their life-styles, even in the face of risk to health. And if behavior change does occur, it is usually gradual, as persons undertake responsibility "in promoting their own health, preventing their own disease, limiting their own illness, and restoring their own health."[43]

Often, however, people are unable to cope with their responsibilities—including that of self-care. They become so overwhelmed that the stress paralyzes them. But what is stress? The term *stress* has been assigned many definitions, depending on the discipline of the writer.

From 1956, when Hans Selye, an endocrinologist, reported his "brilliant and trailblazing studies of the effects of stressful stimuli on laboratory animals, there have been hundreds of inventive experiments on human and animal subjects."[44] These studies have demonstrated that both the threat and the actual use of either psychic or physical stressors produce physiological reactions in vital organs. Based on this kind of information, diverse definitions for stress have developed. For example, stress is defined as "an individual's psychological response, largely mediated by the autonomic nervous system and the endocrine system to any demand made on the individual."[45] Another definition is: "A condition of tension within an individual which occurs as a response to one or more stressors."[46]

All tension is not derived from negative situations. Stress is produced by a wedding as well as by a divorce, by the birth of a child as well as by the death of one, by graduation as well as by dropping out of school. Problems arise when people must adjust to too many events. Most of the time, however, when reference is made to stress, it is to the anxiety produced by negative circumstances.

During World War II a Baptist missionary mother and her six children were passengers aboard an Egyptian ship bound for Africa. There they hoped to join the father at his mission post.

Midway in the ocean, enemy guns shelled the ship. In the panic the mother managed to keep her children together. Eventually she guided them down ropes into a lifeboat, not knowing that the lifeboat too had been shelled. As soon as the boat filled with passengers, it began to sink, spilling all of them into the water. As the children bobbed around in the water, the mother took control. "John! Betty! Chris! Ann! May!" she commanded, "all of you, float!" Every one of them, having been taught strict obedience, floated. The children ranged from fifteen years to a babe in arms. Keeping the baby in the circle of her arms, the mother paddled around, encouraging and commanding them until she had them in a circle. Now she could watch each one and keep strict control.

"Now, let's sing!" came the next command. Above the

roar of the bone-chilling water, the children obeyed. Their voices rose in song—"Jesus Loves Me, This I Know," and "God Will Take Care of You." And God did take care of the Christian mother and her children. The crew of a German radar boat took pity on them and took them all aboard.

In order to do your best, you need to prepare for the tasks you will undertake. The mother in this story had prepared herself and her family very well. She had taught her children obedience. She knew that they could float. She herself knew how to swim. And she knew how to function under stress. She had no energy left for panic—she had herself and six children to care for. She also had provided well for them physically. They were all healthy, so each was able to climb down the ropes into the lifeboat. But above all, she had taught her children to know Jesus, so they were able to sing of His love and care.

That mother was not able to prevent the Egyptian ship from being shelled. She was not able to provide her children with seats in a lifeboat. She was not able to protect them from the ordeal of being in the ice-cold water. But she did her best—and her best was enough. I suggest to you that this Christian mother was no stranger to the text: "A thousand shall fall at thy side, and ten thousand at thy right hand; but it shall not come nigh thee."[47]

In order for you as a Go-getter to do your best, you must not only prepare yourself educationally and maintain a healthy mind and body, you must also learn to know God. Because only by knowing God can you be of service to Him and to your fellowman.

Service to God and Fellowman

Love and service go hand in hand. "For God so loved the world, that he gave his only begotten Son, that whosoever believeth in him should not perish, but have everlasting life."[48]

If you want to be of service to someone, help him to help himself. The essence of a Chinese proverb underscores this idea: If you give an individual a fish, he will eat fish today. But if you teach him to fish, he will eat fish forever.

Serve your friends by exposing them to alternate ways of performing different tasks. Remind them of the importance of time and that how they use their time can determine eventual glory or gloom.

Some years ago my husband took our family to the White House Restaurant in Worcester, Massachusetts. There I saw these words:

Take Time

Take time to *Work*—
  it is the Price of Success.
Take time to *Think*—
  it is the Source of Power.
Take time to *Play*—
  it is the Secret of Perpetual Youth.
Take time to *Read*—
  it is the Fountain of Wisdom.
Take time to *Worship*—
  it is the Highway to Reverence.
Take time to be *Friendly*
  it is the Music of the Soul.
Take time to *Dream*
  it is Hitching your Wagon to a Star.
Take time to *Live*.

This distribution of time gives anyone a real head start.

A little help—rationally directed and purposefully focused at a strategic time—is more effective than more extensive help given at a time of less stress.

As Go-getters, we cannot afford to do less than our best, because—

> Christ has no hands but our hands
>   to do His work today.
> He has no feet but our feet
>   to lead men to His way.
> We are the only Bible
>   the careless world will read.
> We are the sinner's gospel.
>   We are the scoffer's creed.
> We are the Lord's last message
>   given in deed and word.
> What if the lines are crooked?
>   What if the print is blurred?
>   —*Author Unknown*

To this point, *The Go-Getter* raises many important questions. In chapter six—"Jesus First"—you will find suggestions that will assist you in finding answers to some of these questions.

Jesus First

*"Seek ye first the kingdom of God, and his righteous-
ness; and all these things shall be added unto you."*[49]

As children of God, if our supreme goal is to see His
kingdom established, we will want to become the best of
whatever we are, so that we will be prepared to lead others to His kingdom. This is one of the reasons we are told:
"Study to shew thyself approved unto God, a workman
that needeth not to be ashamed."[50]

Many never stop studying, because they realize that we
are never fully educated—that at best we can only be in
the process of *being* educated. Education is an ongoing
process. In this chapter I speak to those who have yet to
complete their education—those who look forward to college and perhaps post-graduate study. Perhaps I can prepare you—to some degree—for what to expect. We will
consider the following areas:

1. Educational levels
2. Academic ranks
3. How to succeed in your present educational project

To help society develop and function on a higher plane,
one is not compelled to obtain an advanced degree. Other

69

modes of preparation may not earn degrees but are practical. Some modes provide theoretical knowledge, yet others provide both theoretical and practical knowledge.

When one is evaluated primarily on the basis of practicality, his level of performance is the determining factor. However, when one is evaluated on both a theoretical and a practical level, he is often expected to have diplomas, certificates, or degrees.

After completing high school, some go on to college. During counseling sessions I have found that students usually decide on majors the same as that of some professional whom they know. They take these professionals as role models. But often a student hasn't the faintest idea of the educational preparation or time necessary to obtain that level of education. One parent reported to a hometown newspaper that her child was studying to be a psychiatrist—the student was a college freshman! So for the few who might benefit, I will include an outline of average years of preparation needed to fulfill requirements for specific degrees.

After completing high school in America—or, in the British system, after completing five "O" (Ordinary) levels or a combination of five "O" and "A"(Advanced) levels—a student goes on to study for an average of four years in college. Upon successfully completing the courses in his chosen field and fulfilling other requirements of the college, he receives a Bachelor of Arts (B.A.) or a Bachelor of Science (B.S.) degree. This is sometimes referred to as an undergraduate degree. In most fields, beginning or entry-level jobs are available for persons with this degree.

In some areas the Associate of Science degree (A.S.) or the Associate of Arts (A.A.) degree may be obtained by two years of study beyond high school. For example, there is the A.S. degree in nursing. This degree has the ladder advantage, in that later a person may study for the B.S. in nursing and continue on to the Master's or Doctoral level. Or a person may obtain the A.S. in secretarial science and continue on to the B.S. degree.

Some, however, decide to specialize in a particular area within their field. For example, if they are studying for a bachelor's degree in chemistry, they may take courses such as general chemistry, organic chemistry, biochemistry, qualitative analysis, and physical chemistry. But in studying toward the master's degree, they will select one of these subjects—perhaps biochemistry—for in-depth study and research. After successfully studying for an average of two years, they will receive a master's degree. Positions are usually available for persons with this degree, and many individuals terminate their formal studies at this point.

Others may continue their education toward a doctoral degree by specializing in a still smaller area. For example, such a person might focus on isolating an antibiotic, as did Alexander Fleming. After doing much in-depth study of what has been already accomplished in that small area, the student does further research and makes a contribution to the field. This usually takes an additional three to four years, and—upon successful completion—a doctor's degree is granted.

There are many different kinds of doctoral degrees. For example:

Ph.D.—This degree means "doctor of philosophy," but the student's field may be art, biology, chemistry, English, and so on.

Ed.D.—This degree means "doctor of education," and consists of several educational specialties, the broad categories of which are elementary, secondary, and higher education—each with its own subspecialties such as reading or administration.

Many other doctoral degrees are available. Some of these are given after persons receive the master's degree, but others do not require this. For example, the Doctor of Social Work (D.S.W.) is usually preceded by the Master of Social Work (M.S.W.). Likewise, the Doctor of Public Health (D.P.H.) is preceded by the Master of Public Health (M.P.H.).

The M.D. degree (Doctor of Medicine), however, is not preceded by a Master in Medicine. The M.D. is the beginning degree in medicine, and the general structure of most such programs is that a student completes a bachelor's degree, spends four years in medical school, then one year as an intern in a hospital setting. Upon successful completion of this program, the M.D. degree is granted. However, several specialties exist in medicine, and the number of years necessary for a given specialty varies from two to six years.

Remember that whether you are preparing for a degree or not, you are constantly studying. Those who are preparing for degrees probably study more intensely, but most people daily learn something new. Check up on yourself today to see if my statement is correct.

Academic Ranks

Academic institutions differ somewhat in their criteria for academic rank. Importance is attached to these qualifications:

1. Preparation (degrees earned)
2. Teaching experience (in general)
3. Number of years teaching in the particular organization
4. Research involvement
5. Publication of scholarly articles or books

6. Off-campus involvement—community, state, federal, international
7. Peer evaluation

Academic ranks include:
1. Instructor
2. Assistant Professor
3. Associate Professor
4. Professor
5. Tenured Professor

How to Succeed in Your Present Project

The ABCs for success are similar in any educational project, regardless of the level:
1. Acceptance: Accept yourself for what you are. Remember—you are a child of THE KING—not a king.
2. Belief: Believe in yourself. You must know yourself in order to believe in yourself. It is as Socrates taught, "Know thyself."
3. Choice: Choose wisely that goal toward which you strive. It must be your choice, not someone else's.

How to Apply:

Whether you are applying for a job or for admission to a college, remember that the application is your representative. Answer all questions correctly—and write neatly and legibly. Develop your answers on other paper and then transfer them to the application form.

As a high-school graduate applying to Oakwood College for admission, I followed the method I have just outlined for you. And guess what! It netted me the position as secretary to the college president, F. L. Peterson, from my first to my last day at Oakwood College.

If you are given extra space for comments, use that space for positive comments or leave it blank. Do not use it to make excuses for any shortcomings you may perceive in yourself. And if you expect to be at a different address between the date of application and admission, make appropriate provision for receiving your mail.

Schedule:

Congratulations! You have been accepted to a college. Follow the school calendar. Try not to arrive on campus a day earlier or later. Why risk a negative start? It is registration time. Follow the schedule. Use the resources: information desk, residence hall assistants, the counseling service, the department in which you plan to register.

Some people say, "I want information straight from the horse's mouth." But if you need assistance, your first contact should *not* be the registrar, the dean of students, the academic dean, or the president of the college. You are a very important person, and these people will be happy to serve you, but why not save them for when you have a *big* problem.

Now comes the day for which you have long waited— the first day of classes. *Be on time for your classes.* You should have consulted the map during registration and become acquainted with the location of your classes. A teacher's opening remarks or overview of a course is critical to your success in the course. Pay strict attention. Learn when to speak and when to listen—the cues will come from the teacher. Observe whether you are in a lecture class or a discussion class and act accordingly.

Responsibility:

You are responsible for fulfilling the requirements for

the course as explained in the course outline or syllabus. Be sure you are on time to receive yours.

Check the schedules for all of your classes, and develop your personal schedule. Then budget your time. Set hours for worship, study, classes, work, recreation, and socializing. If you do this, you will always be available for your friends—but within *your* time frame. Have you ever heard the saying, "If you want to get something done, ask a busy person?" Soon your friends will be saying, "Let's plan it for between 7:30 and 8:30 so Julie will be able to attend."

Setting Priorities:

In developing your personal schedule for the first quarter or semester, you find that you have an English paper due Monday, October 28; a project for cultural anthropology due Tuesday, October 29; an examination for introduction to social work also for Tuesday, October 29; and a Bible examination for Friday, November 1. But you have been aware of these assignments since September 2.

Now, what are your plans? How are you going to handle these assignments? You are well on your way to success in that you are not haplessly and helplessly floundering around. You are the promise of the present, and you are enroute to a successful future.

Suggestions? You can take care of any developing problem by being aware of your responsibilities. Therefore plan your program by prioritizing your assignments and then implementing your plan. For example, you will need to complete your anthropology project ahead of schedule and have it ready to submit on the assigned date. Do *not* report in class that you have finished your project unless the teacher suggests that it would be helpful to receive completed projects prior to the due date.

As for the English paper, if you have to complete the typing over the weekend, fine. But be sure you have written the paper earlier. You will then have part of the weekend, plus Monday and Monday night, to review for the introduction to social work examination—and Wednesday and Thursday to *review* for the Bible examination.

Not bad, if you have carefully analyzed your syllabi, developed your own schedule, and budgeted your time. However, if all these assignments should sneak up on you over the weekend in question, you would be paralyzed. Go-getters plan, prioritize, and prepare. Do not ask for extensions unless you have been sick. Exercise self-discipline, and get your work done on time.

Suppose your teacher does not distribute a course outline or syllabus? Show the teacher this volume, *The Go-Getter,* and say that when you read this, you understood that all teachers gave advance notice of class expectations. Your teacher won't want to place you in a disadvantaged position.

Grades:

What about grades? In most colleges, percentage grades are translated into letter grades—and those letter grades are equated with points.

Grades	Points per semester hour
A	4.0
A-	3.7
B+	3.3
B	3.0
B-	2.7
C+	2.3

C	2.0
C-	1.7
D+	1.3
D	1.0[51]

To graduate from an accredited liberal arts undergraduate college, you must complete 128 semester hours with a cumulative grade-point average of at least 2.0. That means that if you were to receive an "A" in a three-hour course—which is equal to 12.0 points, and a "C" in another three-hour course—which is equal to 6.0 points, you will have a "B" average—which is equal to 9.0 points.

Remember—all of your grades are important and are taken into account and reported each semester. Use your intelligence. Mistakes are always possible. Check your grades. Save your examinations until you receive a more permanent document such as a transcript.

One more suggestion on grades. When a student begins getting low grades in the first year, it becomes increasingly difficult to increase that grade-point average (GPA). So start out right—always above a "C."

By the way, the same year-classification system is used in college that was used in high school.

First Year—Freshman
Second Year—Sophomore
Third Year—Junior
Fourth Year—Senior

So not everything will be new to you. Most people complete their work in four years. But if for any reason you need to take less than a "full" load any given term, classes are taught during the summer.

Many people hide behind the fact that the Lord called uneducated men to be His disciples. These usually forget

that He was their teacher for three years. So keep studying. If consecrated, uneducated people can win souls for
Christ, how much more might consecrated *educated* people?

Finances:

Oh! About paying your expenses! You have several al-
ternatives available to you:

1. Study now—pay later: bank loans
2. Pay as you go:
   a. Use your own savings. You may have something
      saved from your summer work between high-
      school graduation and the start of college.
   b. Accept assistance from your parents, your church,
      and all well-wishers. They want to invest in you.
   c. For American citizens, grants (free money) are
      available, as are low-interest government loans.
   d. For students from other countries, check with
      your Department of Education. Most countries
      have educational packages for students who wish
      to study abroad.
   e. Work is usually available on the college campus
      during the summer. With careful planning and
      explicit communication with the college, some
      students are able to work full time. Part-time em-
      ployment is also available during the school year.
   f. The college usually has scholarships for which
      many students may qualify. Often donors stipu-
      late a GPA of at least 2.0.

I am certain that by now you realize this book is written straight from my heart—not just from my pen. Let me
share further insight into financing your education.

If you are interested in obtaining an education, you must be willing to sacrifice. Although I won academic scholarships at Harvard University, it still took me ten years after I received my doctor's degree to repay my educational loans. Why? I was not poor enough to qualify for free money (scholarships/grants)—and I was not rich enough to pay my way through! But as long as you are making good grades, low-interest educational government loans are almost always available.

Plan your work, and work your plan—and remember, "Seek, and ye shall find; knock, and it shall be opened unto you."[52] Let Jesus be first in all your undertakings, and you will be able to eliminate the words IF and NEVER from your vocabulary.

My last chapter—"Recipes" will provide you with some final helpful hints on becoming a real Go-getter.

Recipes

"We know that all things work together for good to them that love God, to them who are called according to his purpose."[53]

This is a "how-to" chapter. But rather than focusing on standard solutions and pat answers to problems, we need to place our full confidence and trust in God. We need to be sure that our love for God is independent of the outcome of our daily activities. We need to be prepared to accept His answers to our requests—whether those answers be Yes or No. And we need to keep in mind not only who we are, but *Whose* we are.

The topics pursued so far in these chapters remind us that there is a place for every worker in God's vineyard— that although our beginning responsibilities may be less than grand, they are nevertheless important—that we must begin where we are, using talents we possess—and that if further educational preparation is necessary, we must strive until we have attained to our highest potential.

Any approach to the accomplishment of the above tasks must be multifaceted. In this chapter I will provide some suggestions.

Very often I have heard students remark, "The most

81

difficult teacher is a new teacher"—one who has just completed an advanced degree. As a trainer of teachers—both at the Center for Urban Studies at Harvard University and also at Atlantic Union College—I have tried to discover the cause for this perception of new teachers. One of my discoveries is that new teachers tend to teach students that which they themselves have most recently learned—and most of the time such material is too advanced for the students.

When some people attain a high educational level, they forget that they have grown and that growth means that earlier their own understanding and knowledge was less than it now is.

This "how-to" chapter is included for those readers who may find these recipes useful because they have not already mastered all that others have. I will try to keep this information simple. Although many of you may already know and may have already tried these recipes, remember that you did not always know all that is included here. So give others, who are still growing, a chance to gain from this information.

Many of you who read this book may already have completed all the "formal" education you plan to obtain in life. But the real Go-getter realizes that not all real education is found in the classroom. The Go-getter is always striving for excellence and knowledge—and that is the message of this chapter.

In the pages ahead, we will focus on the following areas:

1. The sharing of happiness with family, church, and community.
2. The place of thankfulness.
3. Recipes for successful living.

Sharing

The secret of joy is

*J*esus first,
*O*thers next,
*Y*ourself last.

While you are developing your life goals, you may be spreading happiness in your family, church, and community. How? By identifying a need and filling it.

Several years ago while I was still a student, one of my many jobs was that of planner for a low-to-moderate-income housing complex. My responsibilities ranged from getting the department of public works to install directional signals at crosswalks—(so that residents would be able to safely cross the busy thoroughfare)—to providing for health services. It took many people, from different walks of life, to accomplish such a task. It wasn't possible to erect a clinic there, even though the nearest hospital was not comfortably close. So I identified a need and started to fill it. I began selection for first-aid training for at least one individual in every building (six apartments per building). I did not remain in that position until the total plan was implemented, but the authorities saw merit in the idea.

However, I did remain in another community long enough to implement another idea which filled a need. I felt compelled to mention this because it was a felt need in the home, the church, and the community. My husband and I felt that our children would benefit from the same kind of education we had obtained. But there was no church school, although there were many children in the local church. We not only motivated the church members, but we built the school with our own hands. My husband became its first principal, and that church school is now the largest and fastest growing in the whole conference.

As you decide to be of service to others, you will be able to find many needs. Select one and fill it. In filling needs, people share and spread joy by giving of their knowledge, their understanding, and their humor. Since you are aware that you cannot share more than you have, let me summarize how you may obtain much:

1. Know where you are and where you want to be.
2. Structure your goal.
3. Develop intermediate goals—these will enable you to experience success more often.
4. Do not settle for mediocrity. Remember, you are a Go-getter.
5. Set your own standard, if necessary, and turn your job into a position.

The Place of Thankfulness in Success

"Were there not ten cleansed? but where are the nine?"[54]

Scripture records that as Jesus passed through Samaria and Galilee, He entered a certain village where He met ten men who were lepers. They shouted to Jesus, since they couldn't come near, and asked Jesus to have mercy on them. Jesus told them to go and show themselves to the priest, and as they went, they were cleansed.

Do you think their cleansing was in their showing themselves to the priest? I believe that faith and obedience were ingredients in that recipe for success. Success—cleansing—came to all ten lepers, but only one returned to say Thank You.

I was intrigued as I analyzed the passage (Luke 17:11-19) to note one detail. Just as the lepers had called in a loud voice to make their request, so the healed leper turned back and with a *loud voice* glorified God. Don't be ashamed or afraid to give thanks publicly to God for your achievements. To some that may seem old-fashioned now. Many young ministers have never even heard of the old-time testimony meetings, during which church members openly gave thanks to God. One commentator remarked, "If we cannot be thankful for what we have received, then let's be thankful for what we escaped."

Persons considered successful are often asked questions such as "Where do you get the time to do all those things? You visit hospitalized students. You telephone the elderly and shut-ins. How do you manage?" It could be that these successful people know that the sick and shut-ins depend on them for communication, and they do not want to disappoint them.

We are dependent on God for more than we probably realize. In fact, we take a lot for granted. I can still remember my first air flight, traveling from Antigua to Trinidad to attend high school. As the plane emerged above the clouds, I couldn't help wondering whether we were going to land in heaven—or just where. But I knew that many of the 200 church members had accompanied my family to the airport, and I knew they were all praying for me—so I was not afraid. I knew I could depend on them. We know we can depend on God. But do we sometimes become so complacent that we forget to say, "Thank You, Jesus"?

When floods or tornados happen, people remember to pray for protection. But when everything is going well, we tend to forget that the tides of the oceans would probably submerge the mountains if God's hand did not continually keep the moon 238,857 miles away from the earth.

Let us thank God for what He has done for us—even those things of which we may be unaware. And in particular, let us thank Him for the successes He has given us in our strivings. Too often, though, we thank God but forget to thank our parents, relatives, and others who have helped us, including our government.

Many people—especially parents—do not perform tasks or give assistance in order to receive a reward. But when someone says, Thank you, the giver knows that the attempt to help has been successful.

I'd like to take time right here to say Thank you to some who have contributed toward making my life most meaningful. I want to say thanks to them—or to their relatives.

The late Mrs. Dinah Daley and the New Carmel Church in Montserrat, West Indies. "Aunt Di," as she was fondly called, would prepare the children of the New Carmel Church for three months, after which they would present a Thirteenth Sabbath program in the church. Then she would tour the island with the program. I was one of those children. Performing as children before large and strange audiences prepared us to be Go-getters.

The late Ms. Linda Austin. "Ma Lin" was mother for many teenagers and young adults. As she labored at Caribbean Union College in Trinidad, West Indies, she opened the door of success for many of us.

I am delighted to refer to other mentors who are alive. *Pastor and Mrs. A. R. Haig* were parents to many students in the West Indies, but I was special. Pastor Haig would say, "Sue, you have the potential. You can reach any height."

Pastor and Mrs. S. L. Gadsby in Trinidad. Enid and I were student colporteurs and lived *free* at the Gadsbys' for that summer.

Sister Gadsby was Enid's mentor, and Elder Gadsby was my mentor. Elder Gadsby taught me how to budget both time and money. Enid and I were older than the Gadsby children, and, although we lived with the family, we had no specific chores. They wanted us to spend our time working strictly on our colporteur projects so that we would be successful. Naturally, we were.

Much later at Atlantic Union College I recognized my need for assistance only once, and *Dr. Rochelle P. Kilgore* was there for me. I was a second-semester college freshman. One day the physician told me I was pregnant. In the same breath she said to my husband, "If you really want this baby, you must take your wife home (we lived on the second floor) and put her to bed. For the next two weeks she must leave her bed only to go to the bathroom. At the end of that period you must bring her back to me."

I was registered for a full semester load. In fact, I was in the middle of the semester—too late for a tuition refund of any kind. I went to Dr. Kilgore. She was my only female teacher. She instructed me in detail what to do. "Write two notes," she said, "one to the academic dean, asking for a two-week leave of absence and the other to all of your teachers, explaining your situation and reminding them that for all of last semester plus this semester, you have never been absent from classes or even tardy for any classes. Ask them to support your request to the dean." She continued, "Bring the note to me, and I will sign it first."

The child later born to us, is now a graduate of Atlantic Union College.

As you strive toward being a Go-getter, your pathway will not always be smooth. A support system can be very helpful. A pleasant personality and your home training—

which taught you to say Thank you—will help you
through.

Following are some recipes to success. Understanding
how to use them will make your progress easier.

Recipes

Here are recipes for four kinds of success.
1. Social Satisfaction
2. Healthful Living
3. Educational Development
4. Spirituality

SOCIAL SATISFACTION:

As a Go-getter, if social satisfaction is one of your goals,
mix equal parts of the following elements:
1. Values
2. Tact
3. Understanding
4. Sharing
5. Respect
6. Honesty
7. Cheerfulness
8. Warmth
9. Courage
10. Humility

HEALTHFUL LIVING:

According to Scriptures, threescore years and ten (sev-
enty years) is the lifespan for human beings. A ten-year
study of smoking by British male physicians, confirms
that the smoking of cigarettes is hazardous to health.
Smokers as compared with non-smokers have a signifi-

cantly higher death rate from lung cancer, chronic bronchitis, and cardiovascular disease.[55] "The Surgeon General, in the report *Smoking and Health,* identified cigarette smoking as 'the single most important environmental factor contributing to premature mortality in the United States.' "[56] "Risk consistently increased for both men and women as the daily dose of cigarettes increased."[57] Therefore to give yourself a better chance to live life to the fullest, the following recipe might be helpful:

Smoking—NONE (also avoid nonprescribed drugs).
Foods—Eat to live. Do not live only to eat.
   Fresh fruit and vegetables, grains, and nuts—help to keep you healthy.
   Avoid fats as much as possible.

Sleep:

Although some people need less sleep than others, our bodies are so created that everyone is healthier if his sleeping and waking are scheduled and regular.

"Only since the invention of artificial light sources have human beings attempted on a large scale to manipulate the timing of the sleep-awake cycle to accommodate socioeconomic needs."[58]

It has long been recognized that the hypothalamus is instrumental in the rest-activity cycle and in part of the sleep-wake regulatory system. Nearly ten years ago, a specific area of the brain—the suprachiasmatic nucleus (SCN) of the hypothalamus—was identified as a central neural pacemaker responsible for the generation of the rest-activity cycle.

So, if you are healthy, your sleep-wake regulatory system will help you determine how much of each twenty-four hours you need to spend in sleep.

Exercise:

Exercise is good for the body. With any exercise program you select, begin gradually. You should not attempt to be an Olympian in a week, a month, or even a year. Before deciding on any program, take into consideration the time you have. Develop consistency—taking into account your health, age, and the space which you occupy. Remember that walking is in most cases an ideal exercise.

Self-actualization:

Develop yourself to the fullest. Learning is a lifelong adventure. Keep your brain active.

EDUCATIONAL DEVELOPMENT

College Degree:

Measures	Ingredients
1 cup	Desire
1 cup	Perseverance
1/4 cup	Willingness to delay gratification
1/4 cup	Patience
1/4 cup	Motivation
1/4 cup	Organization
1 cup	Ability to listen and learn
1 dash	Fun

Stir gently, pray without ceasing, and bake for four years.

Getting and Keeping a Job:

Measures	Ingredients
2 cups	Confidence
1 cup	Self-esteem
1 cup	Knowledge
1 cup	Enthusiasm
1 1/2 cups	Motivation
1/2 cup	Courtesy
1/2 cup	Dependability
1/2 cup	Loyalty
1/2 cup	Honesty

Mix well—blend to a smooth finish.

In any recipe that people may decide to follow, ingredients such as self-discipline, creative vision, purposefulness, self-respect, understanding, and a host of other attributes could be included.

Select your ingredients well, and be the first to know whether the recipe works.

SPIRITUALITY

"Eye hath not seen, nor ear heard, neither have entered into the heart of man, the things which God hath prepared for them that love him."[59]

Heaven is the greatest goal for which any Go-getter can strive. "For God so loved the world, that he gave his only begotten Son, that whosoever believeth in him should not perish, but have everlasting life."[60]

Whatever a man sows he reaps. Therefore if we love God and our fellowman, we will find that by giving to others, we receive. Through faith and trust in God, "The Go-getter will get what he goes for."

Footnotes

Introduction

1. Raymond Sill, "Hero and the Coward."
2. Psalm 37:24.

Begin Where You Are

3. Ecclesiastes 9:10.
4. Ina Duley Ogden, "Brighten the Corner Where You Are," *Youth Sing* (Washington, D.C.: Review and Herald Publishing Association, 1977), p. 16.
5. Patrick Mahoney, *You Can Find a Way* (Washington, D.C.: The Institute for the Study of Man, 1982), pp. 102, 103.

Use What You've Got

6. Proverbs 30:28.
7. B. J. and Elizabeth Kaston, *How to Know the Spiders* (Dubuque, Iowa: William C. Brown Co., 1952), p. 7.
8. *Ibid.*, p. 2.
9. *Ibid.*, p. 1.
10. J. F. Tait, G. Pincus, S. M. Willoughby, "A Comparison of the Metabolism of Radioactive 17—Isoaldosterone and Aldosterone Administered Intravenously and Orally, to Normal Human Subjects," *Journal of Clinical Investigation,* vol. 46, no. 5, 1967.

11. Nancy M. Tracy, "The Courage of Meg Casey," *Reader's Digest,* January 1984, pp. 81-85.

12. Joseph E. Gould, *Challenge and Change* (New York: Harcourt, Brace, Jovanovich, Inc., 1969), p. 378.

13. *Ibid.,* p. 387.

14. *Ibid.,* p. 386.

15. See 1 Kings 19.

16. Matthew 25:14, 15.

IF Is Not Part of Your Vocabulary

17. Proverbs 22:29.

18. See Matthew 9:20-22.

19. Acts 3:1-6.

20. Esther 4:16.

21. Egon Larsen, *Men Who Shaped the Future—Stories of Invention and Discovery* (New York: Roy Publishers, 1954), p. 64.

22. *Ibid.,* p. 56.

23. *Ibid.,* p. 63.

24. Ellen G. White, *Christ's Object Lessons* (Washington, D.C.: Review and Herald Publishing Association, 1954), p. 334.

25. *Ibid.,* p. 356.

26. *Ibid.,* pp. 359, 360.

27. *Ibid.,* p. 332.

Never Is Not a Word

28. Philippians 4:13.

29. James F. Calhoun and Joan Ross Acocella, *Psychology of Adjustment and Human Relationships* (New York: Random House, Inc., 1978), p. 26.

30. Proverbs 22:6.

Your Best Is Enough

31. Matthew 25:21.

32. James 1:5.

33. Patrick Mahoney, p. 144.

34. Andre Maurois, *Life of Sir Alexander Fleming* (New York: E. P. Dutton & Co., 1959).

35. Deuteronomy 6:6, 7.

36. See Ellen G. White, *Patriarchs and Prophets* (Mountain View, Calif.: Pacific Press Publishing Association, 1958), p. 592.

37. Proverbs 22:6.

38. 3 John 2.

39. Marshall Becker, "Psychosocial Aspects of Health-Related Behavior" in Freeman, et. al., *Handbook of Medical Sociology* (Englewood Cliffs, New Jersey: Prentice-Hall, 1970), pp. 253, 254.

40. Marshall Becker, *The Health Belief Model and Personal Health Behavior* (Thorofare, New Jersey: Charles B. Slack, Inc., 1974).

41. David A. Hamburg, et. al., *Health & Behavior Frontiers of Research in the Biobehavioral Sciences* (Washington, D.C.: National Academy Press, 1982), p. 111.

42. *Ibid.*, p. 33.

43. Lowell S. Leven and Ellen L. Idler, "Self-Care in Health," *Annual Review of Public Health*, vol. 4, 1983.

44. Sol Levine and Norman Scotch, *Social Stress* (Chicago: Aldine Publishing Co., 1977), p. 3.

45. John Atrochi, *Abnormal Behavior* (New York: Harcourt, Brace, Jovanovich, Inc., 1980), p. 685.

46. Sydney H. Croog, "The Family As a Source of Stress," in Levine and Scotch, *Social Stress* (Chicago: Aldine Publishing Co., 1977), p. 21.

47. Psalm 91:7.

48. John 3:16.

Jesus First

49. Matthew 6:33.
50. 2 Timothy 2:15.
51. Atlantic Union College Bulletin, 1983-84.
52. Matthew 7:7.

Recipes

53. Romans 8:28.
54. Luke 17:17.
55. Brian MacMahon and Thomas Pugh, *Epidemiology, Principles and Methods* (Boston: Little, Brown, & Co., 1970), p. 238.
56. U.S. Department of Health, Education, and Welfare, 1979a, in Hamburg, ed., p. 39.
57. U.S. Department of Health and Human Services, 1980b, in Hamburg, ed., p. 39.
58. U.S. Department of Health and Human Services, Hamburg, ed., p. 111.
59. 1 Corinthians 2:9.
60. John 3:16.